Hi there,

Growing up as the oldest of 12 kids I watched my mom creatively "hack" her way through life. She had a gaggle of little kids, and our house had tile floors that needed regular cleaning. So she would pour soapy water on the floor and give us rags and we would would go to town, playing AND cleaning! It sounds crazy today, but it was her original mom hack.

Today, as the mom of 7 kids of my own, I have to admit I've never done that one. But I have come up with plenty of hacks. And my friends, and moms and dads I meet, have so many great ideas that I love to incorporate into my mom life. So I've gathered my own personal favorites here for you.

Every parent has a favorite hack to make her life easier or her family's life better. What's yours? Email me: vanessa@chatbooks.com or tweet me @vanessaquigley. I can't wait to hear from you!

Xo,

Vanessa Quigley
Co-founder, Chatbooks

I **LOVE** every tip in this book, but I did play favorites—you'll find them noted with this heart! ♥

one

Kitchen Confidential

You are what you eat... so what's for dinner?

> WHEN I COOK, I ALWAYS MAKE TWICE AS MUCH AS WE NEED FOR DINNER AND PUT THE OTHER BATCH IN THE FREEZER OR SAVE FOR LATER IN THE WEEK.

I love serving delicious meals to my family, but every day three times a day?! The innocent question, "What's for dinner?" can make me lose my cool if I'm not prepared. Growing up in a big family I'm used to dealing with massive quantities of food so I'm not afraid to cook up 5 lbs of ground beef or chop tons of veggies at once if it saves me work later. I cook double of everything when I can. A little more work now saves mama's sanity later!

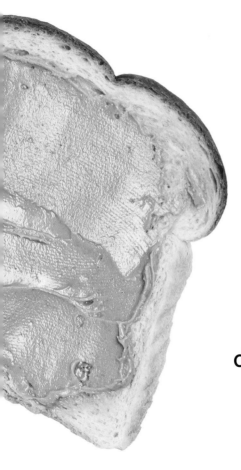

I make a month's worth of school lunch sandwiches, bag them, and freeze them. Each morning, I throw them in lunchboxes. They defrost by lunch while keeping everything else cold!

Vanessa Hunt
@wanderlust.crew

My hack is knowing when to order take-out. As a mom who loves to cook, I used to feel guilty if I wasn't always cooking for my family every day. But I am also a working mom and that can't always happen. That's where take-out comes in!

Tiffani Thiessen
star of Dinner at Tiffani's

Cut children's food with a pizza cutter! I'll never forget seeing my friend do that when he and his wife had us over for dinner. I took a mental note and now do it with my own kids. ❤

Kara Miller

Did you know you can put oatmeal in the crockpot the night before? Use the rice setting, enter how many hours you want to delay it, and it will be ready when you wake up! It's been life changing during the school year for breakfasts.

Hanna Madsen

Park next to the shopping cart return! It means I don't have to carry everyone into the store to get a cart and better yet, when we come out I don't have to go far to return the cart.

Arrin B.

Crock pot liners will change your life! They're food-safe plastic bags you put in the crock pot before adding food. You just toss them when you're done, so there's no mess to clean up.

Brittany H.

I buy a bunch of $5 rotisserie chickens from Costco, then shred and freeze them. Then I just pull out a little bit as I need it.

Tiffany Jensen

When we're home, kids eat what we're all eating. When we're traveling, kids get to eat what they want. Who wants to spend vacations fighting with your kids? By allowing junk food to be an exception out of the house, it takes the pressure off of parents and lets the kids indulge a bit.

Virginia M.

Use muffin tins instead plates to entice kids to eat: simply put a different food in each cup. Our favorites: grapes, berries, oranges, apple slices, cheese cubes, deli turkey, crackers, carrots or other veggie & dip, cubed avocado, yogurt, chocolate chips, popcorn, almonds, and raisins.

Erika Peterson
@cleansimpleeats

"MAKE GREEN SMOOTHIES USING FROZEN SPINACH."

Rachel H.

Always keep a couple of your baby's favorite foods on hand at dinner time -- for us, it's blueberries. That way, when she loses interest in eating her chicken or broccoli, we can tempt her to stay focused with a couple of blueberries.

Elizabeth Segran
staff writer, Fast Company

I have a standing Fresh Direct order for milk, eggs, frozen waffles, etc. that's delivered to my door once a week. And I get my kids involved in the decisions too—just like if we were pushing a cart through the aisles and we were talking about what foods to get.

Ann Shoket
Author of The Big Life *and former Editor-in-Chief of* Seventeen Magazine

I have a bin in my pantry labeled "lunch" that contains all the nonperishable items we use in our kids' school lunches. Everything is already in individual serving sizes and makes the mornings much smoother.

Rian Krommenhoek

Freeze your kids' leftover Halloween or Easter chocolate. Eat it throughout the year or pull it out and chop it up to use when baking.

Jordan Page
Fun Cheap or Free

Think about dinner during breakfast. I always do a quick mental rundown in the morning, so I know if I need to pick up something last minute at the store or if there is any prep that I can plow through when I have a few free minutes during the day.

Kelsey Nixon
Food Network star and author of Kitchen Confidence

Grown-up Secrets

From date night to dry shampoo... here's what makes parent life really work

DRY SHAMPOO FOR THE WIN! WITH A FEW SPRAYS AND A QUICK BANG WASH, YOU'RE GOOD TO GO FOR UP TO 5 DAYS. JUST FIND A CUTE SHOWER CAP!

Do you ever fantasize about life before kids? Just me? I love my family with all of my heart but man, life was easier when I only had to worry about myself! Of course I wouldn't have it any other way, so I've found shortcuts to get the most out of each 24 hrs. My husband may not love my big purple shower cap, but not washing my hair every day saves me four hours a week. Winning!

"DON'T B
TO ASK FO
HIRE MO

E AFRAID
R AND/OR
RE HELP."

Alison Faulkner
@thealisonshow

Take more pictures than you think you need, and capture the everyday along with planned events. Write down the funny things your children say so you can read it back to them as they get older. This motherhood thing looks different on everyone and one "hack" I've found most valuable is to do your best to capture it all.

Jacqui Saldana
@babyboybakery

With two kids under 3 and a busy, demanding job, I'm always craving a little "me-time" by the weekend! My husband and I each get a weekend afternoon "off-duty." From 1-5pm on Saturday, I can do whatever and he does the same the next day.

Zhou Zhang

My husband and I do date night on Thursdays—it lets us skip both the Friday crowds and the competition for babysitters!

Camille Anderson

I assign "categories" to each day—Monday is library day, Tuesday is the pool, Wednesday is art day, etc. It cuts down on decision making and it helps me keep track of everything.

Lisa Valentine Clark
actress and "Real Mom" of Chatbooks commercials

I schedule work phone calls during drive time. It's a great time to get them done!

Gwendolyn Gardner
President, Simply Chickie

When you order a happy meal at Mcdonalds, instead of Gogurt or apple slices ask them for DOUBLE FRIES! One for your kid, one for you. Face it, your kid isn't going to eat the fruit or yogurt anyway and now you get a reasonably-sized portion of those heavenly fries.

Natalie Bussio

I used to be TERRIBLE at falling asleep with my makeup on. Then I realized I have to be in the bathroom to bathe my kids each night, so I wash my face while I am in there! Voila, life changing. ♥

Jenny A Moore

"I SAVE ALL **BABYSITTERS** IN MY PHONE WITH "**BABYSITTER**" IN FRONT OF THEIR NAME, SO I JUST OPEN MY PHONE AND SEARCH "**BABYSITTER**" WHEN NEEDED."

Allyson Downey
founder of weeSpring and author of Here's the Plan

Listen to your children—they are truth tellers! They see you more keenly, and are more invested in your success than anyone else on the planet.

Whitney Johnson
author of Disrupt Yourself! *and* Dare, Dream Do

I've stopped trying to multi-task. I found that instead of being able to do two things at once, I was doing everything poorly. I now try to do only one thing at a time: when I'm at work, I focus on work. When I'm at home, I don't work. Instead, I'm with my family and am fully engaged.

Susan Petersen
CEO Freshly Picked

I find it easy to get engulfed in the "what ifs" of life, which can lead to discontentment. Instead, commit to a two-year plan: ask yourself: "Does every member of my family have the resources they need to succeed and be happy during the next two years?" It forces you to think about each person individually and what they need to flourish (space, finances, community, etc). Then you commit to the next two year plan, rinse, and repeat.

Amanda Goetz

3

Play's the Thing

Because parenting is fun... except when the kids are bouncing off the walls.

AFTER YEARS OF HOARDING ALL OF MY BELOVED SCRAPBOOKING SUPPLIES I'VE FINALLY TURNED EVERYTHING OVER TO MY KIDS. NOW THEY CAN ENTERTAIN THEMSELVES FOR HOURS!

I have a high tolerance for chaos, but even this mama has her limits! When I have work or a project I need to do but my kids need me, I have them work/"play" right alongside me. Back in my scrapbooking days they would happily cut paper and draw while I worked, but I guarded my massive trove of supplies—stickers, markers, papers, punches, stamps— for "mom only." Recently though I surrendered all those to supplies to my kids and they feel like they've hit the jackpot!

Install a Nest Cam security camera in the basement so you can keep an eye on the kids from your phone when you're somewhere else in the house. If you're worried about privacy protection, don't sign up for the option to save your footage in the cloud. Without that part, you just have a live feed that you can tune into any time.

Heather Kennedy Hudson

Switch out a regular light bulb for a disco one and any time becomes party time!

Ashlee Chappell

I take turns with my kids hiding (and then finding) a few toys in a room. We use binoculars and call it a safari. For my older kids, I put out 8 to 10 items and they have to try to memorize them. Then I take away one of the items and they have to identify what's missing. Sometimes we turn the tables and I'm the one who has to figure out the missing item.

Jennifer Beyer Toone

We keep a running "push-up score-board" on our fridge—not to beat each other, but to see our counts increase!

Kara Haught
co-founder of Raising Wild

Create a designated "kids work area" in your main living area. We've set up a little art desk for our son with all of his supplies stored underneath. He can color, write notes, and create awesome art, all while staying close to his dad and me.

Beth Anne Schwamberger
Founder of Brilliant Business Moms

My baby loves to be at my ankles while I'm getting ready for the day, so I started doing bath time in the morning as play time. I fill the tub with bath paints, bubbles, and toys—it keeps her entertained for a long time.

Hailey Devine
@haileydevine

When life gets busy, the house is messy, or we're all a little grumpy, I turn the music up really loud in our kitchen and start dancing. Within a few minutes, everyone is smiling again and life is good. ♥

Shea McGee
@StudioMcGee

Bring little sticky notes on flights: your baby can stick them all over the tray in front of the seat, then pull them off.

Brittany Hayward

Fill a rimmed cookie sheet with rice, cars, and little dump trucks—it keeps toddlers entertained for hours!

Sarah Banks

"BEST EVER: PUT A BLOW-UP BOUNCE HOUSE IN THE BASEMENT."

Camille Anderson

four

4

Sleepy Time Solutions

Your kids hate it and yet you can never get enough: here's how you both can win.

BEDTIME STORIES WORK LIKE MAGIC EVEN WHEN SOMEONE ELSE READS THEM! MY KIDS LOVE AUDIOBOOKS AND LOVE FALLING ASLEEP TO THEIR FAVORITE AND FAMILIAR STORIES.

I have fond memories of my mom reading books to us at bedtime. We'd all gather in her room and she'd read while we started falling asleep. Yet when I tried this with my own kids I was the one to fall asleep—while I was reading! (Yes, I'm that tired.) But then I discovered audiobooks and it's a win-win! Even my teens love them, and now they're the ones nodding off during story time and I save myself the embarrassment of slurring though *Harry Potter*.

Throw a towel in the dryer a couple minutes before the kids get out of the tub. It keeps them calm and they get sleepy quickly. ♥

Ellie Jones

When we have a big day ahead, like a day of travel, we create a story about the upcoming day to prepare our kids. For example, instead of a long grueling day of flights, we tell a story about an exciting adventure on a magical plane that's taking them to an amazing destination!

Jessica Gee
@thebucketlistfamily

Don't make your bedtime routine too hard to replicate! Make it something you can do anywhere—home, grandma's house, hotel, etc. We do PJs, brush teeth, prayer, hug and kiss, bed.

Leah Ward

Sound machines. I have no idea how or why people get through the baby years without them. All of that tiptoeing around and cursing the neighbor's dog can be solved with one beautiful ocean track!

Cara Brook
founder of Maskcara

To make bedtime easier, I do "sleepytime balls." If my kids go to sleep without getting up, crying, or stalling, then in the morning I give them one puffy pom pom ball that we put in a mason jar. When the jar fills up, there's a prize. If they don't go to sleep right away, I take one out.

Heather Mildenstein

five

Birth, Baby, and Beyond

Because there are some things you don't necessarily expect when you're expecting.

I'LL ADMIT IT: WE NEVER STARTED WARMING UP BOTTLES FOR OUR BABIES. THEY BECAME USED TO ROOM TEMPERATURE BOTTLES, AND THOSE LATE NIGHT FEEDINGS WERE SO MUCH EASIER!

I had LOTS of baby experience as the oldest of 12. By the time I graduated from high school I honestly thought I knew it all. Ha! The naivety of youth! But I did pick up one trick from my mom that saved me, especially during late night feedings for seven kids: never warm a bottle. My babies were conditioned to not be picky and grew to enjoy a room temperature or even cold bottle.

Instead of giving my little ones baths, I put them in the shower with me in their Bumbo Floor Seat—cleaning the Bumbo and the baby at the same time!

Kimmy Crosby

I hooked up Phillips Hue lightbulbs in the nursery and set them on a dim, glorious color. Instead of being greeted by stark white light at 3 am, I was able to feed my son under gentle spa-like lights that eased me (and him) right back to sleep.

Shala Burroughs

Make your hubby go get you whatever the heck you want to eat after delivering your baby. It took me four kids to realize I had the power to say, "Go get me misoyaki salmon and tuxedo cheesecake from Cheesecake Factory because I don't have to eat this hospital crap!"

Vanessa Raine Hunt

Layer two fitted sheets on a crib or mattress: when your child has a middle of the night blow-out or accident, you already have a fresh set of sheets on the bed. ♥

Veronica Andrews

My husband brought an air mattress to the hospital when I went into labor, and the nurses told him he was brilliant!

Mikaela Hart Lennberg

I don't just carry an extra set of clothes for my babies—I carry a whole extra outfit for myself, because I often get the brunt of a diaper blowout! I also bring a grocery bag to put those dirty clothes in.

Ali Hynek
@ali_hynek and founder of Nena and Co.

Give yourself permission to take care of yourself and do things that make you happy. When you're happy, you are a better mom! For example, I got a lot of judgement when I went back to work two weeks after my son was born, but I realized going to the office for a few hours made me happy.

Lorena Garcia
co-founder Bloguettes

6

Household Hints

Clean is a state of mind.

> "
> ALWAYS MAKE THE
> BED! IT ONLY TAKES
> A MINUTE TO DO,
> BUT WHEN I WALK
> INTO MY ROOM
> AFTER A LONG AND
> SOMETIMES HARD
> DAY, SEEING A WELL
> MADE BED MAKES
> ME FEEL LIKE
> I'VE GOT MY ACT
> TOGETHER.
> "

When I was little I couldn't fall asleep if my room was a mess—or rather, if I could see the mess. Before getting in bed I'd stuff all my toys into my closet or under my bed so they were out of my sight. A "clean" room gave me peace of mind. As an adult I still value the "clean look" and occasionally still stuff my clutter in a closet now and then until I have time to really deal with it. That's why I swear by making the bed every morning. I feel peace knowing that at least that one corner of the house is in order!

For me, the key to getting laundry done is doing one load a day. I put a load in at breakfast and after work I switch it to the dryer. I fold it straight out of the dryer and my kids put it away. Every Sunday, I put on a TV show and I pull out clothes that need ironing.

Morgan Bandley Thomas

I keep a scrubber brush filled with equal parts dish soap and white vinegar in my shower. Before I get out, I do a quick scrub on the shower then rinse with clean water. The shower always looks sparkling clean and stays free of tough water marks and soap scum.

Lyndsey Cosgrave

The Roomba robot vacuum is worth the price. I can get my kids to pick up quickly if I tell them I'm going to start it up. They freak out if they think the Roomba is going to suck anything up that it shouldn't!

Kelli Woffinden Radmall

We set up a weekly rotation where each of our 3 kids is completely responsible for a certain chore for the full week: walking and feeding the dog, or loading the dishwasher. ♥

Becky Higgins
founder of Project Life

We stopped using that pesky top sheet—now we just pull up the comforter or quilt and the bed is made.

Shanda Munns

"MY TWEENS AND
MONEY AND I HA
WANT TO DO. EITH
TO GIVE THEM MO
THEM TO **DO TH**

TEENAGERS WANT
VE JOBS I DON'T
ER WAY, I'M GOING
NEY, SO I JUST PAY
E JOBS I HATE."

Erika Anderson

Car Talk

Whether you're traveling across town or across the country, your second home should be as comfortable as your first.

I KEEP A $20 BILL HIDDEN IN MY CAR FOR EMERGENCIES— LIKE REALIZING YOU FORGOT YOUR PURSE WHEN YOU'RE OUT OF GAS!

Every mom knows what it feels like to live out of her car. We spend so much time hauling kids and their gear around that it really starts to feel like a second home. But nothing kills the joy ride faster than realizing you've forgotten your wallet and need gas, or a Big Gulp. I've learned to keep a $20 bill hidden in my car for any such emergency.

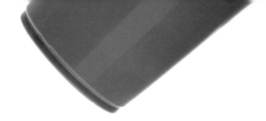

I keep a hair tie on the stick shift of my car in case I need one last minute. #YouNeverKnow

Nikole M.

Store a potty chair in the trunk. It's like a constantly available bathroom stop for toddlers when you are traveling across country (or just across town). 'Nuf said.

Sashanna C.

I leave a chenille sock in the glove compartment, wear it like a sock puppet, use it for a quick dusting, and then toss it in the wash. ♥

Helena F.

I keep a stack of plastic cups in my car to hand food back to my kids when we have to grab a quick dinner in the car or for snacks on road trips.

Shelly Hyde
co-founder of Raising Wild

I love using libraries as pit stops during long drives. They're much more enjoyable than your typical rest stop because most libraries have kid play areas, nice bathrooms, and even snacks.

Shari Medini
co-owner of AdoreThem.com

Keep baby powder in the car when you're headed to the beach. At the end of the day, rub baby powder on your kids' sandy skin and watch the sand just fall away—no scrubbing (or tears) required!

Christine Munns

8

The Organized Life

A place for everything and everything in its place.

> APPS TO THE RESCUE! I USE TECHNOLOGY TO MAKE ORDER OF THE CHAOS IN MY HEAD AND HOME.

I'm a wannabe minimalist. I dream of clear open spaces and easily finding everything I need. But it's hard to minimize with a family of nine! Kids need lots of stuff and keeping it all in order can feel impossible. But I can at least try to keep my head decluttered! I rely on a few apps to help me feel organized: Evernote helps me keep track of important information and documents and Venmo helps me keep settled up with sitters/tutors/and kids' allowances.

I stopped trying to organize my photos and make albums: instead, I connected my social media and phone camera roll to Chatbooks, and now I automatically get a new volume every 60 photos.

Tara Shields

I've found that a hanging cubby organizer by our front door helps corral all of the "stuff" my kids need for extracurricular activities. I labeled the organizer by day, and put whatever needs to go to school or relates to that day's activities in the cubby for that day. For example, Wednesday is library day, so the library book is in the Wednesday slot. All that my kids have to do is look in that cubby as they walk out the door.

Jenny A Moore

We have a morning "check off chart" with all the things my kids need to do before they catch the bus. It helps them get everything done and they love checking things off!

Emily Munns

I have several buckets throughout the house. Any time I come across a random toy during the day, it all ends up in the closest bucket. At the end of the day, the kids help me empty the buckets and put everything away. It helps keep the house tidy throughout the day, keeps me from stepping on loose legos, and when one of the kids comes asking if I've seen a toy, all I have to say is, "Check the bucket." ♥

Melissa Cook

Our family has a weekly "Power Hour" early on Friday evening: we each conquer one chore that comes up irregularly, like getting the car's oil changed, organizing a closet, or booking vacation flights. At 6pm we're done and feel extra productive as we head into the weekend!

Megan H.

I got sick of late fees when our library books got mixed in with the books we own. I put one shelf in my children's room that's only for library books. It's right next to their beds so it puts the books on display and they read them often because they are so accessible.

Ashlee Chappell

Put kids in neon clothes when you travel and are on vacation—neon hats for snowy climates, neon t-shirts for the beach. It makes it much easier to spot kids in crowded places!

Melanie

I keep an ongoing list of things that need to be done around the house and the amount of time it should take to complete each task. Then I set a timer on my phone and see if I can beat it!

Tiffany Munns

I recently put a Lazy Susan inside my fridge: great for seeing those condiments that hide in the back of the fridge.

Natalie Norton
@natalienorton

"I PRE-MAKE STACKS OF LITTLE LUNCH NOTES FOR MY KIDS."

Jessica K.

Healthy Habits

How to do the right thing, even when it's hard to fit in.

> **"**
> I CREATE PHONE ALARMS FOR EVERYTHING FROM 'HUG KIDS' TO 'PLUG IN PHONES TO CHARGE.' SOME GO OFF EVERY DAY AND SOME I JUST FLIP ON WHEN I KNOW I'LL NEED A REMINDER LATER.
> **"**

When it comes to teaching my kids the importance of healthy habits like washing hands, brushing teeth, and good nutrition I take my job very seriously. A healthy and strong body is very important. But so is our emotional health and one way I boost the good vibes is to hug more. I sometimes get busy and distracted with to-dos and work that I forget to hug my people. So I set alarms on my phone throughout the day to remind me to stop what I'm doing and hold on to the people I love the most.

If your kids ask for sugary cereals or other treats at the store, make a game out of reading the labels and finding the one with the lowest sugar so they'll want to take that winner home with them!

Cailey Tonks

Give kids lots of choices. For example, "Do you want me to do the teeth brushing or do you want to do it?" Make sure you give only choices that you are okay with.

Chanel Beazer Termeer

With five kids and lots of after-school activities, we are sometimes in the car until the evening. We often do our evening family devotional routine in the car on the way home instead of at dinner. It saves time, and everyone pays attention!

Dr. Amy Osmond Cook

I save all of my no-brainer kitchen chores for when my daughter is doing her homework at the kitchen table. I'm in the same room and can easily answer her questions as they come up, while still getting my own work done! ♥

Gwendolyn Gardner
President, Simply Chickie

My kids get to pick four snacks per day from a basket on our table. Normally they snack at 10am, 1pm, 4pm, and before bed. I've found this is way better than constantly being asked for a snack.

Emily Mudroch Roberts

Pair your own fitness activity with one of your child's sports practices: my daughter's ballet school is right near a park, so every Saturday morning I drop her off and go for a run while she's in class.

Lynn Andriani

I get fully ready for the day every morning before the kids go to school, so I'm ready to start my day when they are out the door (and not tempted to crawl back in bed).

Heather Munns

I apply sunscreen before we get outdoors, or especially to the pool, mostly so they aren't so anxious to run and play, and bypass mama's sunscreen bath.

Lisa Richards
Skin Boss

"I GIVE MY DAUGHTER ONE TOOTHBRUSH TO HOLD WHILE I BRUSH HER TEETH WITH ANOTHER. **NO MORE WRESTLING OR TEARS.**"

Aubri Darton Bradford

Happier Holidays

Adding more fun to the festivities.

> **OUR TOOTH FAIRY KEEPS OUR KIDS GUESSING. THEY NEVER KNOW WHAT THEY'LL GET OR WHEN SHE'LL PAY HER VISIT!**

I love carrying on holiday traditions
from my childhood—like breakfast in bed for all girls on Mother's Day to celebrate mom AND future mothers. But some just evolved—like our generous tooth fairy that comes when she pleases (or remembers!). She's fickle but fun! I have an alarm on my phone that if I remember to set, she rewards the toothless child with a big handful of change from our coin cup.

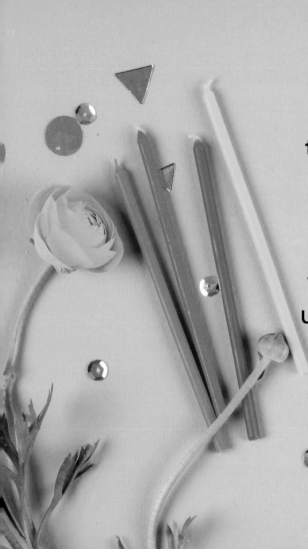

We start celebrating birthdays on the first day of the birthday month and have a special treat each day until the actual birthday. It's anything from dollar store trinkets to a love note.

Mindy Weedall

On birthday mornings, we tape a ton of streamers across the child's bedroom door and they have to bust through it when they wake up.

Jackie Thompson Kontoes

We do videotaped birthday interviews for each kid—they're so fun! We also do a mini photo shoot for the birthday kid. ♥

Ashley Raney

For my husband's 30th birthday, I got him 30 presents and wrapped each individually. Some were small, like his favorite candy and some were bigger, like gift cards. It was so fun for him to open all those presents and we spent the day using up a lot of the gift cards!

Juli Picklesimer

Always keep thank you/birthday/teacher cards on hand along with $10 Starbucks gift cards—the same goes with kids' birthday presents. You'll always be prepared on the spot!

Keenan Sanders

"LAST YEAR MY NEIGHBOR GAVE US THE GIFT OF **"TIME"**— PAPER PLATES, CUPS, NAPKINS, AND UTENSILS FOR OUR FAMILY SO WE WOULDN'T HAVE TO DO DISHES ONE NIGHT."

Jessie Alexis Evans

For Valentine's Day, I "heart attack" my boys' rooms—I cut out dozens of paper hearts and write things that I love about them.

Kelsey Brems Hill

For Christmas stocking stuffers or Hanukkah gifts, buy candy that you can't get everyday like Japanese or European brands. It feels much more special than regular candy!

Heather Norton

We used to have a hard time finding gifts for my in-laws until all of the siblings got together and decided to open a savings account for them to use for a trip/destination. We wrote a letter and gave them the account info. Now every Christmas and birthday we all just keep adding to it.

Jared-Amy Card

We make a short holiday bucket list each year, where we jot down all of the things we really want to do as a family. It includes all those things that we'd feel sad if we got to the end of the holidays and missed! Then we take that bucket list and put it on the calendar: breakfast with Santa, looking at lights, etc.

Emily Ley
creator of The Simplified Planner and author of Grace, Not Perfection